Discovering

POND LIFE

Colin S. Milkins

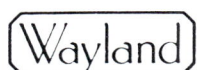

Discovering Nature

First published in 1989 by
Wayland (Publishers) Limited
61 Western Road, Hove
East Sussex BN3 1JD, England

© Copyright 1989 Wayland (Publishers) Limited

British Library Cataloguing in Publication Data
Milkins, Colin
    Discovering pond life.
    1. Ponds. Organisms
    I. Title   II. Series
    574.92'9

    ISBN 1–85210–601–8

Typeset by DP Press Ltd., Sevenoaks, Kent
Printed and bound in Italy by Sagdos S.p.A. Milan

All photographs from Oxford Scientific Films

Editors: Clare Pumfrey and Clare Chandler

Cover *A stickleback lies in wait to eat the eggs laid by a common blue damselfly.*

Frontispiece *A leopard frog leaps from a leaf into the pond.*

Contents

1
Introducing Ponds

Warm water and lots of nutrients in ponds allow plants, such as waterlilies, to grow well.

What is a Pond?

A pond is a small area of still water, usually no more than two or three metres deep. There are several differences between ponds and other freshwater **habitats** such as lakes, rivers and streams. In summer, ponds are warmer than lakes because they are shallower, and do not take so long to warm up. Unlike a lot of lakes, ponds are often found near or on farmland. Some of the **fertilizer** that the farmer puts on the surrounding fields is washed into the pond when it rains. This fertilizer increases the amount of **nutrients** in the pond. Plant growth is much greater in a pond than in a lake because ponds are warmer and have more nutrients in them.

The water in a pond does not flow along as it does in a stream. For this reason, ponds contain living things

Streams contain more oxygen than ponds because the water is better aerated. Stream water looks white where it mixes with air.

Ponds are less **aerated** than streams, which means that there is less oxygen dissolved in the water. Pond animals are, therefore, used to living in water with less oxygen. Many of the stream animals that need a lot of oxygen would soon die if placed in a pond.

that would not be able to survive in fast-flowing water. For example, the tiny green **algae** that sometimes turn ponds green in summer would be washed away in a stream. Many of the small animals that live in ponds, like the water scorpion, would not be able to cling tightly to stones, and so they would be swept away.

It is tiny green algae like these that make ponds in summer look green.

How Do Ponds Form?

There are several ways in which ponds can form. In the past, a pond would have been dug in a village to supply drinking water. In the nineteenth century, during the **Industrial Revolution**, mill ponds were created by damming a stream or river. The water from the mill pond was used to turn a water wheel, and the power produced by the wheel was used to drive machinery. Ponds were often dug in the corners of fields to provide water for cattle or sheep. In

Ponds were often made when a river was dammed. The water was used to drive water mills, like this one in Virginia U.S.A.

Australia, ponds for this purpose are called farm tanks. Although man-made, all of these types of pond have lots of living things in them.

Not all ponds are man-made. Where water from a spring collects in a hollow and drainage is slow, a pond can form naturally. As long as the spring does not dry up, this type of pond will exist for many years. Other types of pond may only last a few days. If there is a lot of rain, a dip in the ground may fill up to form a very shallow pond that looks just like a large puddle. These short-lived ponds contain **organisms** which must be able to grow and reproduce before the water disappears. Their young will have to adapt to survive the dry period until it rains again.

Many ponds in Australia form when rivers flood. The flood water collects in billabongs. These are narrow stretches of water several

Ponds were often dug near villages. They are no longer used by people but are now havens for wildlife.

kilometres in length but only about 100 m wide. As the billabong dries out, small ponds, teeming with life, are left behind.

The Pond Community

No matter how a pond forms, it is quickly invaded by many living things. **Aquatic** insects will fly in from neighbouring ponds. Other insects whose young live in water, will lay their eggs in and around the pond. Seeds of plants are carried to the pond on the feet of water fowl. Even fish eggs and small mussels can be introduced to a pond in this way. The mussel holds on to a piece of the bird's foot by pinching it between its shells, and then, when the bird settles on another pond the mussel releases its grip and drops off.

After a few years the newly-formed pond will contain a thriving community of plants and animals. The members of the community depend upon one another in many ways. For example, animals cannot make their own food and so they have

Flying insects such as these mating dragonflies will lay their eggs in water.

to rely on plants and other animals for their food. Animals that eat mostly plants are called herbivores and the animals that eat the herbivores are called carnivores.

By finding out how each organism obtains its food, it is possible to arrange them in a food chain. A simple food chain could be: microscopic green algae eaten by water flea, eaten by dragonfly **nymph**.

Here the herbivore is the water flea and the carnivore is the dragonfly nymph. If the algae died out, there

This is a typical food web to be found in a pond. It shows that plants and detritus are essential even to the pike because they are the first stage of the food web.

would be nothing for the water fleas to feed on, and no water fleas for the dragonfly nymphs to eat.

As there are so many different animals in a pond, not many simple food chains like the one above exist. Usually, many food chains cross over one another to form a food web. Food webs show that even **predators**, such as pike, newts and frogs, rely finally on plants for food.

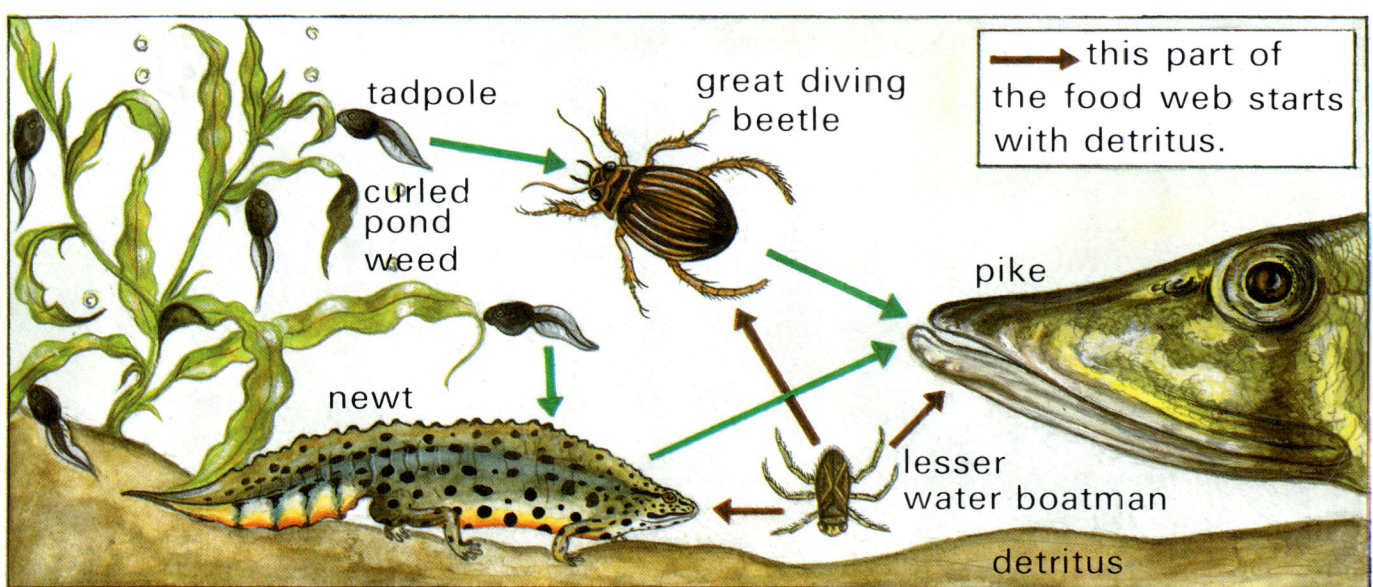

tadpole

great diving beetle

curled pond weed

→ this part of the food web starts with detritus.

pike

newt

lesser water boatman

detritus

The Surface Film

It may seem strange, but there is a tough, rubbery skin on the surface of water. This is called the surface film.

Pond skaters have water-repellent hairs on their feet which help to stop them breaking the surface film and sinking into the water. The weight of these two mating pond skaters is making dents in the surface film.

Several pond animals use the surface film to their own advantage. The pond skater is a common bug which dashes around on the water surface, searching for small animals caught in the surface film. The pond skater has water-repellent hairs on its feet which prevent the surface film from breaking under its weight.

Tiny animals called springtails use the surface film as a trampoline. They

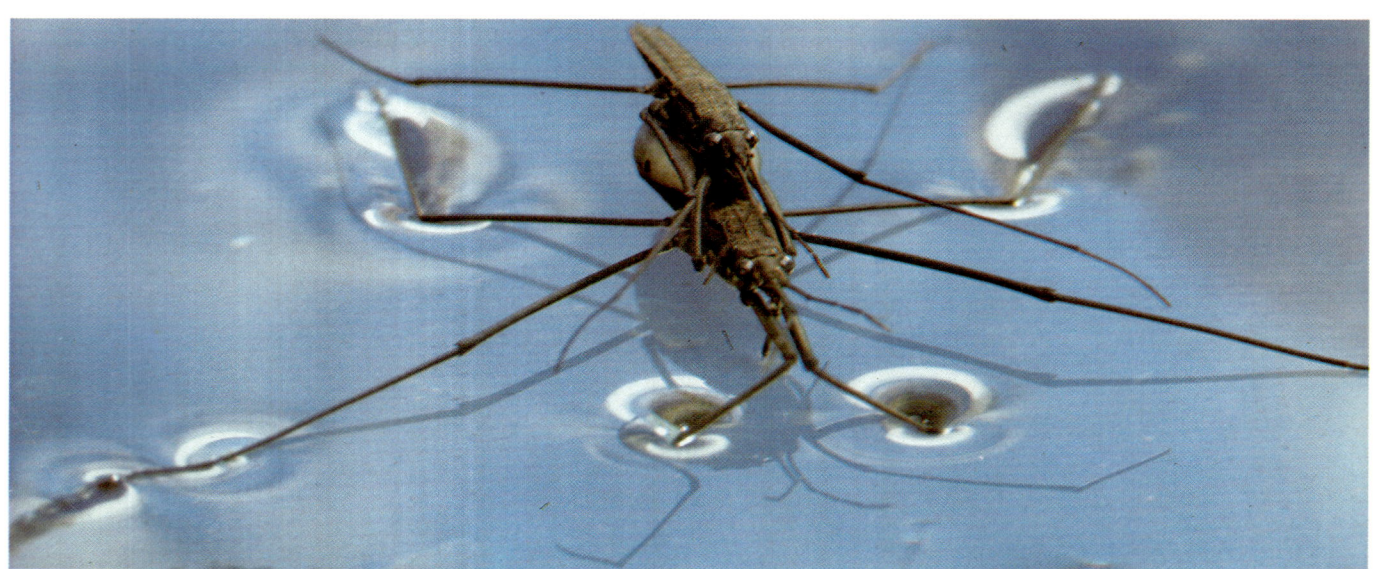

have a springing organ on the hind end and, if a group of these animals are disturbed at the water's edge, they bounce up and down. This behaviour makes it very difficult for a predator to capture them.

The raft spider can sense vibrations in the surface film in the same way that land-living spiders feel vibrations in their webs. This large spider sits motionless on a floating leaf with one of its front legs dangling in the water. As soon as the spider feels vibrations from a struggling insect, it quickly races over the surface of the water and captures its victim.

This raft spider has its leg dangling in the water (on the right), waiting to feel ripples from an insect on the water surface.

The surface film is so strong that it is possible to float a metal needle on it. You can prove this by doing a simple experiment. Pour some water on to a tray and allow it to settle. Then place a piece of tissue paper on the surface. As quickly as you can, gently drop a needle on top of the paper. The tissue will become water-logged and sink, leaving a needle floating on the water film. Add a little liquid soap to the water. This will destroy the water film and the needle will sink. **Detergents** destroy the important surface film and so pollution from detergents is disastrous to a pond community.

2
Water Plants

Submerged plants give off oxygen bubbles which dissolve in the water.

The Importance of Plants

Sunlight is very important to the pond. Without sunlight all pond life would eventually die. The green plants in the pond use sunlight to change **carbon dioxide** and water into food. This process is called **photosynthesis**.

Photosynthesis not only produces food but oxygen as well. When the sun has been shining on a pond for some time, bubbles of oxygen can be seen collecting around the leaves of plants under the water. Gradually, the oxygen in the bubbles dissolves into the water and is used by the animals in the pond. Plants do not supply all of the oxygen for the pond. A lot is absorbed from the air but it is not enough to keep all the animals alive. Without the oxygen that plants make, many of the larger pond animals would suffocate and die.

Plants are not only eaten when they are alive. They are also a very important food source when they are dead. The remains of dead and decaying plants is called detritus. There are animals in the pond that only eat detritus and they are called detritivores. Most of the food in a pond is detritus and so detritivores play a very important part in the food web.

As the detritus is eaten, the dead plants are broken up into smaller and

These freshwater shrimps are busily devouring rotten leaves in the detritus on the bottom of a stream.

smaller pieces. This process returns nutrients to the water which would otherwise remain trapped in the dead plants. These nutrients nourish other living plants in the pond.

Plants not only provide food and oxygen. They are also important as places where smaller animals can shelter and hide from enemies.

Living in Water

Some plants are well rooted in the muddy **margins** of the pond. For example, yellow flag, meadow sweet, king cup and arrow head are common marginal plants in Britain. The leaves of the arrow head that grow above the surface of the water are shaped like large broad arrow heads, but the leaves below the surface are long and narrow. Leaves of this shape are not so easily damaged by movements in

The marsh marigold is a typical marginal plant. It is also known as king cup.

Water lilies grow in many parts of the world. These white lilies are Australian.

the water. Several other species of plant, such as the water-crowfoot, have leaves that are shaped differently above and below the surface of the water for the same reason.

The water lily has large floating leaves called pads. The underside of a pad is a favourite place for the great pond snail to lay its eggs. The upper surface of a pad is punctured by tiny pores (holes) through which the lily breathes air. Plants that live on land have breathing pores on the under surface of the leaf. The upper surface of the lily pad is covered with a layer of wax so that water cannot collect on the surface of the pad and block the breathing pores.

Many pond plants rely mainly on **vegetative** means to reproduce themselves. For example, duckweed quickly covers the surface of a pond because each tiny plant divides every few days. In the autumn, starch is stored away in the fronds of the duckweed. Starch is heavy and gradually the plants sink to the bottom of the pond where they spend the winter. During this time the starch is used as food, and by the time spring arrives, the duckweed has little starch left and is light enough to float to the surface again.

3
Herbivores

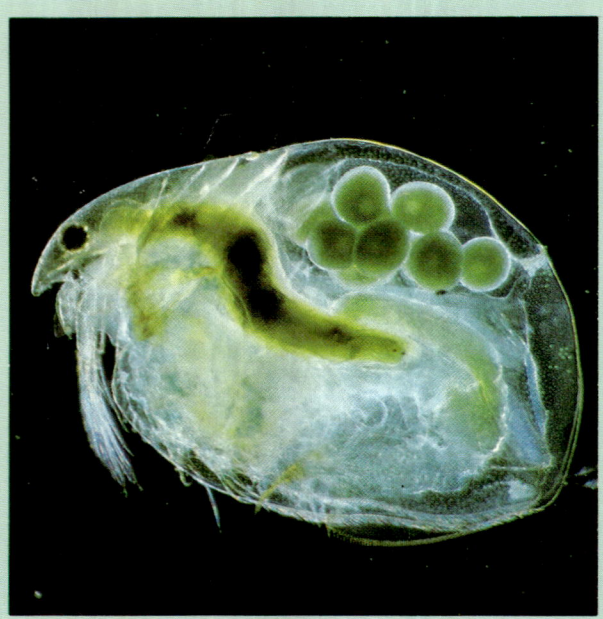

This water flea has been feeding on tiny algae which can be seen in its gut.

Filter feeders

Animals use various methods to strain tiny particles of food from the water. The freshwater sponge feeds in this way by creating a current of water through its body. Special cells in the sponge take out any food particles that may be present in the water. The sponge is really a colony of thousands of single-celled animals. The sponge can be ground up in water to form a 'soup' of single cells. In only a short time, the cells will arrange themselves into a sponge again.

There are several kinds of mussel that filter feed. Thousands of beating cilia (fine hairs) on the **gills** of the mussel draw water into its body. The water is then filtered as it passes over the gills. The particles of food are trapped and concentrated in a ribbon of sticky **mucus**. The particles of food and mucus then enter the

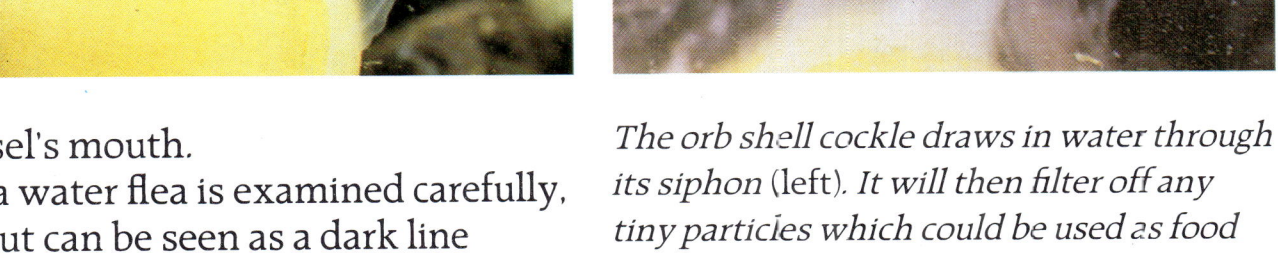

mussel's mouth.

If a water flea is examined carefully, the gut can be seen as a dark line running through the body. If the line appears green, the water flea has been filtering tiny cells of algae from the pond water.

The larva of the mosquito filter feeds by 'combing' the water with the two brushes near its mouth. If kept in an aquarium, the larva can be observed feeding as it hangs from the surface film. Occasionally it will feed

The orb shell cockle draws in water through its siphon (left). *It will then filter off any tiny particles which could be used as food* (right).

by bobbing along, head down, over the bottom.

The tiny fragments of food that these filter feeders eat help the animals to grow. The filter feeders are eaten by larger animals which would not find it worthwhile to eat tiny pieces of food directly.

Scrapers

Pond snails feed by scraping pieces off the soft stems of underwater plants. They have a special 'tongue' called a

The radula, or tongue, of this pond snail can be clearly seen scraping algae from the aquarium glass.

radula. Keep a snail in an aquarium and as it crawls up the glass look closely at its mouth. Every few seconds the radula will be poked out as the snail takes a mouthful of the alga that grows on the glass.

Snails also eat the remains of dead plants such as duckweed. As they do this, the snails help to keep the living plant free from disease. Diseases, which remain in the dead plants during the winter, will be destroyed when the plants are eaten. In the spring new duckweed will then be able to grow free from disease. Some types of pond snails are attracted to the dead duckweed by a special chemical that the plant made when it was alive.

Some pond snails have a lung and need to come to the surface to breathe air. They take in the air through a special pore in the side of the body and not through the mouth as we do.

Snails, such as the great ramshorn snail, have to break the surface film to reach the air. The great pond snail makes quite a loud 'pop' when it comes up to breathe.

Other types of snail, such as the common bithynia, do not have a lung but absorb oxygen directly from the water through a gill. Attached to the body of these snails is a hard, chalky plate, called the operculum. When the snail withdraws into its shell, the

The operculum of this common bithynia can be seen just below its head.

operculum shuts tight over the entrance.

Mayfly nymphs also feed by scraping. They come out at night to eat the algae which grow on the surface of the stones. The adult may-flies cannot feed as their mouths are sealed. They only live for a few days in order to mate and lay their eggs.

Chewers

Some types of caddis-fly larvae resemble caterpillars both in appearance and in the way they feed. They chew up and swallow plant material. Caddis larvae that eat only plants are often called cased caddis. This is because they build a tube, or case, which they drag around with them. They begin making the case by spinning a tube of silk around the body. Then pieces of dead plant, tiny stones or even empty snail shells are stuck on to the silk to complete the tube. The shape of the tube and the choice of building materials varies from species to species. The case **camouflages** the larvae, so hiding it from predators. Also the case may simply make the caddis larvae too painful to swallow.

When fully grown, the larva closes off the entrance to the tube, and over

The cased caddis drags its tube around while it chews on plants.

This caddis case is made from snail shells.

Many large fish, such as tench and carp, chew their food with teeth that are not in the jaw but at the back of the throat. They use their tube-like mouths to suck up plant matter, insect larvae, worms and other small animals which live in the mud. These fish do not always feed on the bottom of the pond. In the early morning and late evening, they come to the surface of the water to gulp down mouthfuls of floating duckweed.

several weeks it changes its form to become a **pupa**. The pupa then bites its way out of the tube and crawls out of the water on to the bank. The adult caddis-fly which emerges from the pupa looks like a hairy brown moth.

Not all caddis-fly larvae are herbivores. Some capture small animals for food. They are called caseless caddis because they do not construct cases.

The tube-like mouth of this mirror carp is sucking up plants and animals from the pond bottom.

Detritivores

There are three common detritivores, or **scavengers**, found in fresh water – the lesser water boatman, which is an insect, the pond slater and freshwater shrimp, which are crustaceans.

The lesser water boatman is a true bug and, like all bugs, has a mouth shaped like a tube. Using the tube as a vacuum-cleaner, the lesser water boatman swims around near the bottom of the pond sucking up liquid detritus. The lesser water boatman is an active swimmer and has flattened front legs which it uses as oars. It can also fly well.

The lesser water boatman sucks up liquid detritus from the pond bottom.

The pond slater, or water hog louse, looks very much like the woodlouse that is found in damp places on land. Pond slaters mate in the spring. The smaller female is carried around by the larger male before mating. By carrying her, the male can prevent other males from mating with her. The pond slater is found where there is a lot of dead plant material, which is its main source of food.

The freshwater shrimp feeds mainly on dead leaves. It is found living in streams and under stones at the edges of lakes. The male, which is larger, carries the female for a few days before they mate. This happens only just after the female has shed her skin. The **fertilized** eggs are carried in a **brood pouch** beneath the female's body until they are ready to hatch. The newly-hatched young look just like the adults, except that they are much smaller.

A small detritivore that can be found in temporary ponds is the tiny bean shrimp, so called because it looks just like a miniature baked bean.

The male freshwater shrimp carries the female around until he can fertilize her eggs.

4
Carnivores

The water spider builds an air-filled bell beneath the surface, to supply it with oxygen while it is under water.

Spiders and Mites

The water spider lives in an air bell which it builds some distance below the water surface. The spider starts to make the bell by spinning a platform of silk between the stems of underwater plants. It collects air for the bell from the surface, and carries it down to the platform, trapped between special hairs on the spider's abdomen. The layer of air makes the spider look silvery as it moves about in the water.

By using its back legs, the spider strokes the air from its abdomen. As the air rises, it is trapped in a bubble beneath the platform. Gradually, as more air is added, the web begins to bulge upwards to form a bell-shaped dome. The spider spends most of its time in the bell absorbing oxygen from the trapped air.

As the oxygen in the bell is used up,

it is replaced by more oxygen which passes into the bell from the surrounding water. Therefore, the spider does not have to make repeated journeys to the surface to obtain supplies of fresh air.

When small creatures become trapped in the silken threads of the platform, the spider runs out and kills the prey with its poisonous fangs. The dead animal is then taken into the bell and eaten.

Young water spiders often spend the winter in empty snail shells. The spider traps an air bubble in the shell by spinning a web over the entrance.

Although the mite is only the size of a pin head, it is a ferocious carnivore. Mites usually attack only sick or injured water creatures. They suck out the body juices of the **prey** with their beak-like mouths. Young mites are **parasites**. They attach themselves to living water insects, such as the water scorpion, and suck juices from the leg joints, where the insect's skeleton is thinner.

Water mites are fierce carnivores, attacking creatures which are ill or injured.

Beetles

The hard, shiny back of a beetle is made up of two front wings. Folded beneath them are the thinner hind wings which are used during flight. Not all water beetles are carnivorous but the spectacular great diving beetle certainly is. The adult beetle can grow to 3 cm in length and will capture and kill newts, tadpoles and fish that are often much bigger than itself.

Like all water beetles, the great diving beetle has to come to the surface to obtain air. It pokes the tip of its abdomen out of the water and lifts the ends of its wing cases to trap a bubble of air beneath them. With its air supply renewed, the beetle quickly dives again.

The female great diving beetle can be recognized by her front wings because they have grooves on them, whereas the male's front wings are smooth. The male's front legs have a flat, round pad on them which in the breeding season becomes sticky. He uses these pads to grip the female during mating. The eggs are laid in water plants and they soon hatch into larvae, which are active hunters like

The great diving beetle can stay for a long time beneath the water. It breathes oxygen from an air bubble which it traps under its wing cases at the surface.

Whirligig beetles dash around on the water surface, but rarely bump into each other.

their parents.

The whirligig beetle owes its name to the way it whizzes around on the pond surface. These beetles are usually found in groups and, although the individual beetles move around at great speed, they never bump into one another. This beetle has two eyes on each side of its head. The lower half of each eye stays below the surface and is adapted to see clearly in water. The top half of the eye which remains above the water surface is adapted to see clearly in air. This type of eye enables the beetle to detect enemies from two directions – fish from below and birds from above – at the same time. The whirligig beetle feeds on insects and other creatures that fall into the pond.

There is a beetle that is found in muddy ponds and makes a very loud screech when caught in a net. The screech beetle, as it is often called, hunts worms that burrow in the mud at the bottom of the pond. The noise is made when the beetle rubs the roughened under surface of its front wings against the sharp edges of its abdomen. A fish would almost certainly spit out this beetle if it screeched when being eaten.

Dragonflies and Damselflies

The nymphs of dragonflies and damselflies have similar ways of feeding. Both are active hunters and they have two large **compound** eyes for detecting their prey in murky water. When the nymph is close enough to its prey it shoots out its 'mask', which is folded beneath its head. The prey is caught by two claws at the end of the mask. As quickly as it is extended, the mask is folded back under the head and the captured animal is eaten. No other insect captures its prey in this way.

Damselfly nymphs breathe dissolved oxygen in the water through three leaf-like gills at the end of the abdomen. These gills are occasionally waved from side to side to stop the water near the gills from becoming stale.

Dragonfly nymphs breathe through

Adult dragonflies do not become brilliantly coloured until they have had their first meal. This is a ten-spot dragonfly from New Jersey, USA.

the **rectum** which is lined with gills. To keep a fresh supply of water passing over these gills, water is gently pumped in and out of the rectum. When alarmed, the dragonfly nymph forces water from the rectum rapidly, which causes the nymph to shoot forwards out of harm's way.

In the spring, when fully grown, the nymph leaves the water by crawling up a reed or grass stem. Its skin then splits and the adult eases itself free. Blood is pumped into the veins of its crumpled wings and so they flatten out and expand to their full size. Once the wings are hard and dried in the warm air, the adult flies off in search of flying insects to eat.

In order to capture their prey in flight, adult dragonflies and damselflies hold their legs beneath their body to form a 'catching basket'. When an insect is caught, it is transferred to the mouth where it is chewed by powerful jaws. It is only after their first meal that damselflies and dragonflies gain their brilliant colouration.

Male dragonflies and, to some extent, damselflies are strongly **territorial**. They can be seen patrolling their territories as they fly

This British four-spotted dragonfly has just emerged from its old skin.

up and down a stretch of river or over the surface of a pond.

Worm-like Carnivores

Leeches can be recognized by their ringed or segmented bodies. They have two suckers at each end of the body. They move by attaching themselves with their suckers and looping along. They also use the suckers to cling to their prey. Some of the larger leeches are able to swim by **undulating** their bodies.

Most freshwater leeches in Britain cannot break the skin of a human and so they cannot suck human blood. Many leeches, for example the horse leech, capture and eat small aquatic creatures. Some suck the blood and body fluids of soft-bodied animals such as snails and mussels.

Some leeches live in the **nasal** passages of water fowl, where they feed on the bird's blood. This type of leech produces a chemical which thins the bird's blood and stops it from clotting. This results in a constant flow of blood for the leech to feed on. This chemical also stops the blood from clotting in the leech's gut too. A blood meal can last a leech several months.

Some leeches suck the blood of animals. This leech is attached to the stickleback by the sucker at the rear end of its body.

Another worm-like creature that hunts its prey is the flatworm. These animals detect injured and wounded animals in the water by special sense cells in the skin. By beating the many tiny hairs on its skin, the flatworm glides effortlessly towards its prey. Flatworms will often try to trap animals by leaving long, sticky threads attached to stones and plants. You may find freshwater animals that have threads trailing behind them. These creatures have blundered through a flatworm snare but have been lucky enough to escape.

Flatworms are able to reproduce without the need to mate. The flatworm attaches both ends of its body to a smooth surface and, by pulling in opposite directions, the body is torn in half. Each half will grow the pieces of the body that are missing. Flatworms can also reproduce by laying fertile eggs in **cocoons** which are then attached to the underside of stones and pebbles.

This photograph shows the inner parts of a flatworm, including its gut.

Carnivorous bugs

Bugs resemble beetles in appearance but instead of having jaws they have sucking mouthparts which are used to suck the juices from their prey. The water scorpion is so called because of its long breathing tube which resembles the sting of the true scorpion. The water scorpion hangs motionless in the water with the tip of its breathing tube just above the surface. When a water creature, such as a small fish or tadpole, comes near, the water scorpion grabs it with its two long claws, and pushes its tube-like mouth through the prey's skin to get at the body fluids.

Another common predatory bug is the greater water boatman, which is

The water scorpion breathes air through a long tube at the end of its body. This one has caught a stickleback.

able to swim very quickly using its two hind legs as oars. Although the greater water boatman actively hunts its prey, it usually hangs motionless upside down from the water surface. If you look closely at the creature in this position you will see that the surface film is broken by rows of fine hairs on its abdomen. This is how a water boatman obtains oxygen from the air. This bug is also known as the 'backswimmer' but it can be made to swim the 'right' way up by placing the animal in a glass jar and then, in a darkened room, shining a light underneath the jar. Be careful when handling this bug as it is capable of giving a painful bite.

The water measurer is a slender, graceful bug that walks on the surface film with slow, measured steps. When it spots suitable prey beneath the water surface, the water measurer quickly stabs it with its tube-like

A water measurer uses its long tube to suck the juices from a fly.

mouth. Then, with great difficulty, the water measurer pulls its prey clear of the water and sucks it dry.

Top Carnivores

Several of the large animals found in and around ponds are known to scientists as top carnivores. This is because these animals are often the last link in a food chain. In the pond, the pike is a top carnivore and is not usually preyed upon by any other animal. Small pike dash about in the pond, chasing shoals of smaller fish. Sometimes the water surface will erupt as hundreds of small fish jump into the air to escape the jaws of the hungry pike.

Large pike lie in wait for their prey. They remain motionless in the water, their patterned sides camouflaging them perfectly. On either side of the pike's body there is a row of small pores which connect to a thin tube

Pike are well camouflaged in the water. This one has just caught a frog.

just beneath the skin. This tube is called the lateral line canal. There are special cells in the canal which enable the pike to feel vibrations in the water. This is how the pike feels the movements of sick or injured fish which can then be hunted down easily and eaten. Larger pike will readily pull ducks and even swans beneath the surface and eat them. In one case the lip of a drinking horse was completely bitten off by a pike.

Several birds visit the pond to find food. The heron comes early in the morning and will slowly walk about in the shallows, hunting frogs, fish, water voles, and even rats. It swallows all of these animals whole. A struggling rat can take an hour or more to swallow.

The lightning-quick kingfisher is another bird which comes to the pond to feed. It plunges into the water to capture minnows or the **fry** of other fish. The kingfisher's waterproof plumage gives the bird a silvery appearance as it swims beneath the water surface.

Kingfishers can quickly catch a small fish.

5
Ponds and Us

Ponds are often filled with rubbish.

Conserving Pond Life

With the introduction of modern water supplies, many ponds are no longer used. They have become filled with rubbish and are generally neglected. However, there are several conservation groups which clean out and maintain ponds. If you join one of these groups you will be able to help in conserving ponds, and learn a great deal from the experts in the group.

In certain areas, ponds gradually become shallower as the dead remains of plants build up on the bottom. If this is allowed to continue, the pond will disappear and become dry land again. So, to keep these ponds, the dead plant material has to be removed regularly.

It is possible to help pond creatures by providing them with a new home. Small, shallow ponds can be created easily in gardens or school grounds.

A pond made with a liner (left). *A year later it looks like a natural pond* (right).

A pond of this sort need not be more than 45 cm deep. The hole can be lined with a special rubber liner, or, if it is quite small, with a piece of polythene, such as a discarded fertilizer bag that has been cut open down one side and along the bottom. Whichever liner is used, there must be no sharp stones beneath it as they will puncture the liner. Put some old logs around the edge to hold the liner down. They will also provide hiding places for pond animals when they leave the water.

The newly-made pond can be left for several years to see how a pond community forms naturally. If you do not want to wait, the process can be speeded up by introducing water, mud, and some plants and animals from existing ponds. You should always obtain permission to do this.

Studying Pond Life

Most pond animals are found clinging to the submerged stems of plants. The best way to catch them is with a net. Push the net through the vegetation fairly quickly, jerking the handle slightly at the same time. This action will knock the creatures off the plants and into the net. Then transfer your

If you collect frogspawn, return the tadpoles to a pond before they turn into frogs.

catch to a white tray – a large ice-cream container or a photographer's developing tray are ideal. Add a little clean water to the tray, not too much or the creatures will be difficult to see. Keep the tray still and soon you will see many animals moving about.

Take a few of the animals home and put them into an aquarium with some pond water. Do not use tap water, as the chlorine it contains may kill the animals. Plant some pond weed to act as a supply of food and oxygen. Many of the smaller creatures that were missed with the net will be present in the weed.

Try to identify as many of the creatures as you can. When the animals in the aquarium have settled down, observe what they are eating. You will need to look very closely in some cases. Using the information you gather, try to construct a food web. Other things to study are the

You may find pond animals like these bean shrimps, which look like tiny baked beans.

ways in which the animals move and breathe. When your studies are over, return the animals to the pond where they were caught. Remember, be very careful when visiting ponds. Always go with an adult who could rescue you if you fell in. Good hunting!

Glossary

Aerated Mixed with air.

Algae (singular: alga) Simple plants that are often very small and live in water.

Aquatic Living in fresh water.

Brood pouch Part of an animal's body where eggs are kept until they hatch.

Camouflage Something which conceals an animal by making it blend in with its surroundings.

Carbon dioxide A gas found in air that dissolves in water.

Cocoon A silky case spun by a larva to protect it as it grows.

Compound eye An eye composed of many lenses. This type of eye is found in insects and crustaceans.

Detergents Strong chemical cleaners, e.g. washing-up liquid.

Fertilized When a female's egg has been joined with a male's sperm, it is said to be fertilized.

Fertilizer A mixture of nutrients, often including manure, that is added to soil to make it richer.

Fry Tiny young fish.

Gills The organs through which many aquatic creatures breathe.

Habitat A place where a community of plants and animals live naturally. Woodlands, lakes, meadows and rivers are all examples of habitats.

Industrial Revolution The period during the eighteenth and nineteenth centuries, when many machines were invented. This led to the development of industry in Europe and the USA.

Margins The edges of a pond that are covered by shallow water.

Mucus A slimy secretion from certain parts of the body.

Nasal Of the nose.

Nutrients Chemicals which plants and animals need to grow.

Nymphs The larvae of dragonflies and damselflies.

Organism The name for plants and animals.

Parasites Animals or plants that live and feed on living organisms.

Photosynthesis The process by which plants make their food.

Predators Animals that hunt and kill other animals for food.

Prey An animal that is hunted by other animals.

Pupa The stage in an insect's life between the larva and adult form. A pupa remains still and does not feed, while inside its protective casing many changes are taking place.

Rectum The part of an animal's gut through which waste is passed out of the body.

Scavengers Animals that feed on decaying plant or animal life.

Territorial Defending a particular area.

Undulating Moving up and down like waves.

Vegetative A means of plant reproduction without the need for a male and female.

Finding Out More

If you would like to find out more about pond life, you could read these books:

J. Clegg, *The Observer's Book of Pondlife* (Warne, 1980).

J. Dyson, *The Pond Book* (Puffin Books).

Linda Losito, *Discovering Damselflies and Dragonflies* (Wayland, 1987).

Mike Linley, *Discovering Frogs and Toads* (Wayland, 1986).

Field Guide to the Water Life of Britain, (Reader's Digest, 1984).

Useful addresses

British Trust for Conservation Volunteers
Royal Zoological Gardens
Regent's Park
LONDON NW1

Index

The numbers in **bold** refer to the pictures.

Picture Acknowledgements

All photographs are from Oxford Scientific Films by the following photographers: G.I. Bernard *cover*, 25 (left), 28, 29, 35, 40, 43; Deni Bown 11; Dr J.A.L. Cooke 22; Stephen Dalton *frontispiece*, 31, 37; Michael Fogden 19; Terry Heathcote 41 (left & right); Michael Leach 8; Alastair Macewen 14, 15; Colin Milkins 16, 17, 21 (left & right), 23, 24, 25, 26, 27, 30, 34, 36, 38; Patti Murray (Animals Animals) 32; Peter Parks 9 (right), 20; Avril Ramage 42; Alastair Shay 12; Ronald Toms 33; Barry Walker 39; Anna Walsh 9 (left); Fred Whitehead (Earth Scenes) 10; M. Wilding 18; The illustration on page 13 is by Lorraine Brown.